A Few Thoughts Abo

by Bob Roddy, OFM Conv.

"What did you give up for Lent?" Tha[...] during Lent when I was a youngster. (Some smart aleck always said, "watermelon," or another outrageous answer.) For many of us Lent was strictly a time of penance, a forty-day marathon of denial with Easter Sunday as the finish line. I suspect that for many people today, Lent is still seen as a test of endurance rather than a preparation for Easter.

While the penitential aspects of Lent are important, we should not neglect the other components of Lent: *prayer* and *almsgiving*. (Our penitential practices are an expression of *fasting*, the other traditional component of Lent.) All of these parts of the lenten season help us journey more deeply into the heart of the paschal mystery of Christ's life, death, and resurrection. This great mystery is celebrated and pondered every time we gather for Eucharist, and often it is revealed in events of our everyday lives. Who of us has not had to die to some part of our self in order to rise to new life? For example, when we ask forgiveness of another don't we have to die to our pride in order that we might rise to new life with the person we have wronged? Conversely, when we forgive another, don't we have to die to our indignation and rise in love to embrace the person who has hurt us?

Today we are deluged with plenty of signs of Easter, from multicolored marshmallow treats, to battery-operated toys that always seem to sell for $19.95. We rarely see any signs of Lent. Consumer culture doesn't lend itself readily to the traditional lenten practices of prayer, penance, and almsgiving. Penance just doesn't "sell." Prayer is not a "growth market," and most people don't have a clue what "alms" are.

Since the Second Vatican Council we have come to a new understanding of Lent and how we might understand these traditional practices. We can **fast** not only in denying ourselves something such as candy, soda, or television, but we can "fast" from bad habits like saying unkind things about others, or using inappropriate language, or being late for appointments. **Prayer** not only can include formal prayers, such as the Stations of the Cross or devotional prayers; prayer can be a spontaneous expression of praise or thanksgiving to God when we have a few free moments in our day. When we are stuck in traffic because of an accident, how many of us think to say a prayer for those involved in the accident? We can give **alms** through the sharing of our time or our gifts with others; we don't always have to open our wallets. A smile and a kind word to another can be a rich expression of alms.

This booklet provides some suggestions for keeping Lent with the family in this post-Vatican II mode. Its aim is to make the traditional areas of prayer, fasting, and almsgiving more available and meaningful for your family, regardless of the size and composition of your family. Because of this, you may wish to do only a few of these activities, or you may need to adapt them to your particular needs and situation. Perhaps you can make this a point of discussion with your family, so that each member feels a sense of ownership of whatever activities you choose to do.

Feel free to be creative with these activities, especially the prayer services. Allow your creativity and the creativity of other family members to emerge. Consider including members of your extended families or neighboring families when possible.

These activities, prayers, and rituals are not in sequence, though some activities, such as "Finding the Hungry," might be ones that you would like to do for the entire season of Lent, and others, such as "The Things Bag," may just be one-time happenings.

The prophet, Isaiah, gives us some good guidance for how to observe Lent, so I'll conclude with his words:

> *Is not this the fast that I choose: to loose the bonds of injustice, to undo the thongs of the yoke, to let the oppressed go free, and to break every yoke? Is it not to share your bread with the hungry, and bring the homeless poor into your house; when you see the naked, to cover them, and not to hide yourself from your own kin? Then your light shall break forth like the dawn, and your healing shall spring up quickly; your vindicator shall go before you, the glory of the LORD shall be your rear guard.*
>
> Isaiah 58:6-8

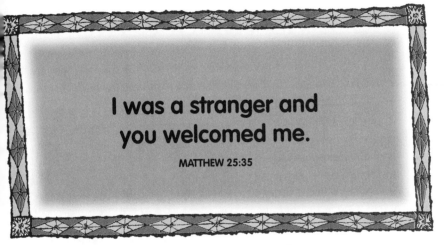

I was a stranger and you welcomed me.

MATTHEW 25:35

Adopt a Catechumen or Candidate

During Lent, families in the Church can frequently be a source of support and love for the catechumens. In fact, a family could "adopt" a catechumen or candidate who is participating in the parish RCIA as a special lenten activity.

Before you begin, talk it over with your family so that everyone knows what you are trying to do and is in agreement. You might discuss some of the challenges that a catechumen or candidate faces as he or she progresses through the RCIA.

Talk with the leader or leaders of the RCIA in your parish, and let them know that your family is interested in helping to welcome a new member. Perhaps one of the leaders or sponsors can arrange an introduction.

You may wish to invite your catechumen or candidate and his or her family

over for dinner or dessert. When you see him or her at Sunday Mass, make a point to stop and ask how he/she is doing. Remember him/her in prayer during mealtime or family prayer time. Drop a note of encouragement to him or her. For Easter, have the family make a special greeting card and send it to this new Catholic.

Rick Potts

Caring for Creation

In the northern hemisphere, Lent occurs during the spring when new life and new growth break forth. The following activities help the family to become more aware of the wonders of creation.

1. Involve all of the family members in preparing or planting a family vegetable garden or flower garden. (Consider inviting a family or person who does not have the possibility of planting a garden to take part in yours.)

2. Get and bless some kind of earth ball to use as a symbolic reminder of ways your family can care for the earth.

3. Discuss the possibility of a weekly or monthly discussion about ways of caring for the earth. Practice good ecology and good recycling efforts around the house.

Digital Stock

**You visit the earth and water it,
you greatly enrich it;
the river of God is full of water;
you provide the people with grain,
for so you have prepared it.**

PSALM 65:9

Let us not grow weary
in doing what is right.

GALATIANS 6:9

family sharing

Focusing on the Positive

1. Everyone needs a pen or pencil and a large sheet of blank paper. Write your name at the top of your paper. Now pass your paper to the person on your right.

2. Look at the name on the paper you now have in front of you. Write down three positive things about that person. Only positive comments are allowed. These can be about anything—the person's appearance, or talents, or character, or temperament, and so on. When all have finished the first paper, pass it to the person on your right, and repeat the process until everyone has the paper with his or her name back.

3. Read what is on your sheet, and then share it with the family. Keep your positive thoughts inventory in a special place in your room.

Gordon Willman

Fasting
OLD AND NEW APPROACHES

Fasting is one of the traditional pillars of Lent. Fasting is not an end in itself, and it must always be done with a commitment to prayer. As we experience the absence of our favorite foods, beverages, or pastimes, and move more deeply into prayer, we will be drawn more deeply into the paschal mystery. Hopefully, the longing that we experience in denying ourselves something or some activity will remind us of our longing for the Almighty.

We also can use this as a time to unite ourselves with our brothers and sisters who go without food, drink, or the many amenities that we have. When we share in their suffering, **their** plight becomes **our** plight. As we experience our longing for some food or drink, we can offer a silent prayer for others in need.

Another way of fasting is to refrain from talking and to take time to listen—and ultimately, to pray—either alone, or with the family, or the community. If at all possible, don't add any other sounds, such as music, radio, or television to your quiet time.

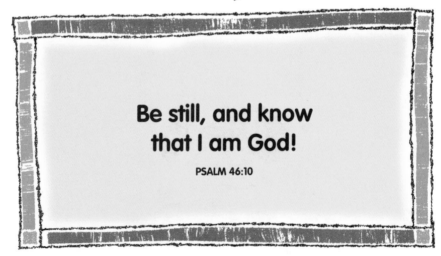

Chris Sharp

Be still, and know that I am God!

PSALM 46:10

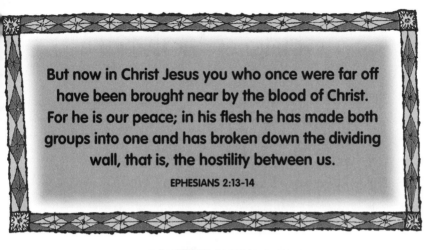

But now in Christ Jesus you who once were far off
have been brought near by the blood of Christ.
For he is our peace; in his flesh he has made both
groups into one and has broken down the dividing
wall, that is, the hostility between us.

EPHESIANS 2:13-14

Wendy Barnes

Peace Box

Decorate a box with pictures and other symbols that show some of the ways and times your household has experienced God's peace and brought God's peace to others. This requires some real discussion, going over your family's history, especially its recent history. Some families have pictures of special family members and friends, of special vacations or places in nature where they have experienced God's beauty, of people who have been their special inspiration in working for others, of people and places where the family has been especially helpful to others.

Symbols of peace can be added to the box, like a rosary, religious medals and small crucifixes, flags from different countries, "love gifts" from family members.

Prayer cards can be added, including those prayer cards of beloved deceased family members or friends who have died recently. Keeping the box in a prominent place in the home, usually on the dinner table, makes it a daily reminder to pray for peace.

Candle Making

Materials Needed:

- Two 1-pound coffee cans
- About 5 pounds of paraffin
- Wired wick
- Broken crayons or old candles
- Scissors
- Cold water

Begin with two, 1-pound coffee cans. Fill the first one with chunks of paraffin (about 5 pounds for fifteen candles), and the second one with cold water. Heat the paraffin until it is all melted but not bubbling. (Broken crayons and old candles can be melted in the paraffin to give color to your candles.)

With a scissors, cut sections of wired wick 8 to 12 inches long (depending upon the length of the candle you wish to make). Hold the top of the wick, and dip it first into the can of paraffin, then immediately into the can of cold water. (Younger children may find it easier and safer to tie the wick to the end of a stick and dip it while holding onto the other end.) The water cools the wax so that it builds up more quickly on the wick with repeated dipping. Continue dipping until your candle is the desired thickness.

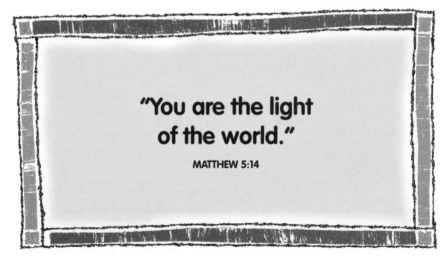

"You are the light of the world."

MATTHEW 5:14

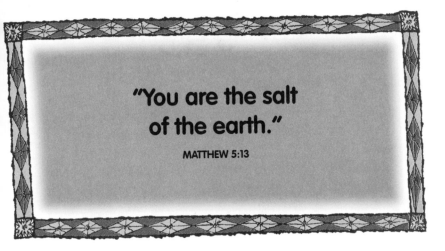

Kolace
(BOHEMIAN FILLED BUNS)

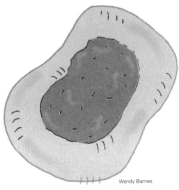

- 1 cup butter or margarine
- 4 eggs, separated
- 1 envelope yeast
- 1/4 cup milk
- 2 cups light cream or evaporated milk
- 1 1/2 cups sugar
- 1 teaspoon grated lemon
- 1 1/4 teaspoon salt
- 5 cups flour
- jam or jelly for filling

Wendy Barnes

In large bowl, cream butter or margarine and add 4 egg yolks, one at a time. Add yeast dissolved in warm milk, 4 egg whites beaten stiff, cream, sugar, salt, and lemon rind. Into this mixture sift 5 cups flour. Beat the dough hard, until it does not stick; cover it and put it in a warm place. When it is double its original size, place the dough, a tablespoon at a time, on a floured board. Roll each spoonful into a ball, and then flatten it like a cookie, about 1/2 inch thick. Make 5 dents in the center with your finger, and fill with jam or jelly. Lightly push up the edges with your finger. Let rise in the pan, brush with beaten egg yolks or cream, and bake in moderate oven (375 degrees) for about 15 minutes or until nicely browned.

Family Light Prayer Service

This prayer service uses the light of a candle and a passage from Saint Paul to help establish a spirit of family charity. You will need a Bible and a candle for the service.

1. Have the Bible set out on a small table. Display it in a way that highlights its appearance. Have a large candle placed near the Bible.

2. Gather the family around this area, and light the candle.

3. Have one family member read from Paul's Letter to the Romans 12:9-21. Ask the person ahead of time so that he or she can prepare the reading.

4. After the reading, remain quiet for a minute or two.

5. Take the lighted candle, and pass it around the family. As each person holds the candle, he or she may pray: **Lord, deliver our family from** _____. (Example: Lord, deliver our family from hurts caused by not listening to one another.)

6. After each person makes their prayer, everyone responds: **Lord, we ask you to hear us.**

7. When all have had a turn, pass the candle one more time. As you pass the candle to the one next to you, thank that person for one way that he or she lights up your family life. Keep going until all have been thanked.

8. Close by praying the Lord's Prayer together.

**Put away from you all bitterness
and wrath and anger...
be kind to one another, tenderhearted,
forgiving one another,
as God in Christ has forgiven you.**

EPHESIANS 4:31-32

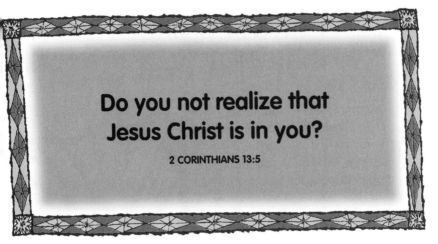

Do you not realize that Jesus Christ is in you?

2 CORINTHIANS 13:5

How Do I Show Respect?

People in India have a simple, yet essentially powerful way of greeting one another. They place their hands together as in prayer and bow to the person greeted. The other person often responds with the same gesture. This sign says, *Amchara*, which means, "I worship the God within you." The gesture is as common in India as the handshake is in the Western world.

The meaning of this Indian gesture contains much wisdom for Christians because respecting and loving the Christ in others is at the heart of what Christian humility is all about. This is what Mother Teresa of Calcutta said she was doing when she ministered to the sick and dying of India. She saw Christ in every suffering person she helped because Christ himself said: "Just as you did it to one of the least of these who are members of my family, you did it to me" (Matthew 25:40).

Discuss among yourselves signs of respect and reverence for one another that you might adopt as a family. You may wish to try doing the traditional *Amchara*, or you might develop a special handshake or greeting. See if you can take a familiar family gesture and put new meaning into it.

Prayer Person of the Week

The terms "enemy," "adversary," "opposition," "renegades," and the like are often used by the media to describe parties at war, political rivals, or other groups who are opposed to one another. When we label people, we stop thinking of them as our brothers and sisters. We find ourselves justified in our actions, some of them quite hostile, because we are dealing with our "enemies."

As you listen to the news, select a person or persons who are definitely in need of prayer and pray for them, by name, at mealtimes and family prayer times. Make them your family's "prayer person of the week." Each family member can select the "prayer person of the week" for Lent. It can be a person who is a national or international or local figure; it may even be someone the family knows, someone whose actions and attitudes may cause the family to think of him or her as an "enemy." Remember this person **by name** whenever you gather for meals or family prayer time.

> But when he heard this, he said, "Those who are well have no need of a physician, but those who are sick. Go and learn what this means, 'I desire mercy, not sacrifice.' For I have come to call not the righteous but sinners."
>
> **MATTHEW 9:12-13**

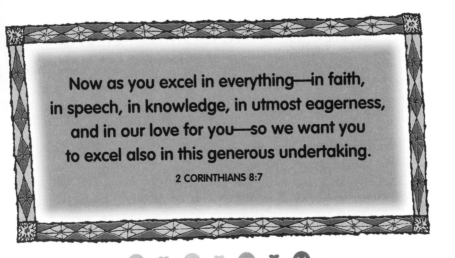

Now as you excel in everything—in faith, in speech, in knowledge, in utmost eagerness, and in our love for you—so we want you to excel also in this generous undertaking.

2 CORINTHIANS 8:7

family sharing

Personal Checkup

As a family, talk about these questions, one at a time. Give each person a chance to answer the questions. If others in the family see you differently than you see yourself, give them a chance to tell you why. Don't argue or be defensive about your attitudes, simply let them be, and accept them as gifts of insight into yourself and your family members.

1. What's my best time of day? What's my worst time of day?

2. Would I like to live with me at my worst time of day?

3. What's my tone of voice when I talk to my family? to my friends? to people I want to impress?

4. Am I generous in sharing my possessions with my family members? with my friends? with my neighbors?

5. Am I generous in sharing **my time** with my family members? with my friends? with my neighbors?

Gordon Willman

Easter Blessing Tree

This project will provide a visual reminder to your family to carry out their lenten resolutions and to practice the love that Christ taught us to live. On Easter Sunday, your Easter Egg Tree can become the centerpiece for your dinner table.

1. Find a tree branch with several strong twigs. "Plant" your tree in an empty, decorated, two-pound coffee container, or a plastic Easter basket.

2. Make a list of special LOVE WORDS that remind you of the joy of Easter. Your words might include: *Jesus, joy, faith, family.* Other love words will occur to you as you are making your list.

3. Obtain some brightly-colored plastic eggs. These are available in discount stores, craft stores, and larger drug stores.

4. Use a magic marker with permanent ink to write a love word on each shell.

5. Open the egg, insert the end of a small piece of yarn, and close the egg.

6. Each member of your family should hang a decorated egg on the tree as he or she does a kind deed or makes a lenten sacrifice. The individual can make the decision when to hang the egg, and does not have to tell the others what he or she did.

7. By Easter Sunday, your tree should be filled with brightly colored eggs that symbolize your family's lenten journey.

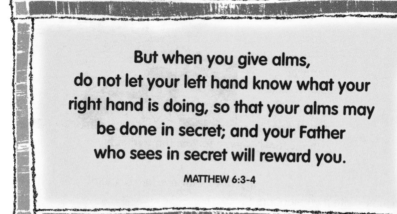

**But when you give alms,
do not let your left hand know what your
right hand is doing, so that your alms may
be done in secret; and your Father
who sees in secret will reward you.**

MATTHEW 6:3-4

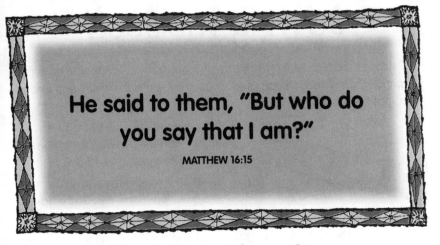

> He said to them, "But who do you say that I am?"
>
> **MATTHEW 16:15**

Who Do You Say that I Am?

Form a definite rotation before you begin this game. Each person, in turn, thinks of a Bible character. When it's your turn, everyone else (in turn) gets to ask you questions in order to guess who your character is. Establish two basic facts about your character before the questioning begins, such as: "I am a Hebrew (or a Gentile, or an Israelite…)" and "I am a woman (or a man, or a child…)." The questions can only be answered with YES or NO. One person can continue asking questions until a NO answer is given, but anyone can interrupt at any time to guess the identity of your character.

(Limit your characters to those biblical people you think everyone in the family is familiar with. Obscure names culled from the pages of seldom-read books of the Bible do not qualify!)

Gordon Willman

Sowing the Seed

Celebrate the God who gives life to all. Plant some seeds for the beginning of spring. You will need a bean seed for each person in the family, and a good-sized pot filled with dirt.

1. After making the Sign of the Cross, read out loud the parable of the Sower and the Seed, Matthew 13:3-9.

2. Ask everyone in the family to answer the question: "How has God made us like the seed?"

3. Have each person take one seed and plant the seed in the pot of dirt. As each person plants a seed, he or she should say: "Lord, help me grow in your love every day."

4. Water the soil, and place the pot in a sunny spot.

5. Watch the green plants grow.

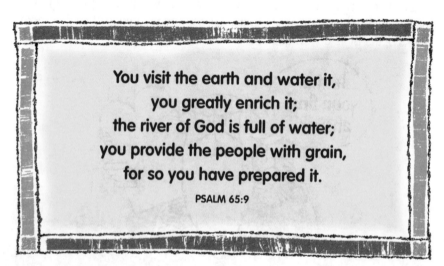

**You visit the earth and water it,
you greatly enrich it;
the river of God is full of water;
you provide the people with grain,
for so you have prepared it.**

PSALM 65:9

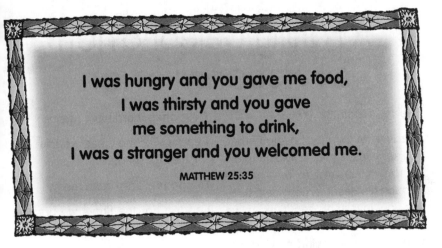

**I was hungry and you gave me food,
I was thirsty and you gave
me something to drink,
I was a stranger and you welcomed me.**

MATTHEW 25:35

Adopt a Country

1. Get a globe or a map of the world; if you have Internet access you can find maps there and print one. Put the map or globe in a room where your family eats together.

2. Check the newspaper, radio, television or Internet for reports on hunger around the world. Find countries where starvation and hunger are major problems. Some suggestions are the following: Sudan, India, Bangladesh, Haiti, Honduras, Ethiopia, North Korea, and Peru. Select a country your family would like to adopt during Lent.

3. When you gather for a meal and after you have thanked God for your food, look at your map or globe and pray for the poor and hungry people of the country that your family has selected. For example, at the end of your meal prayer you might say: "Today, we remember the poor and hungry people in North Korea."

Helpful Web sites:

Catholic Relief Services: catholicrelief.org
World Hunger site: worldhunger.org
Doctors Without Borders: dwb.org

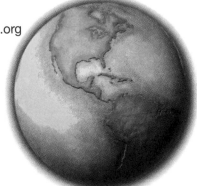

A Family Celebration of Reconciliation

Reader: Psalm 32:1-7

Leader: Let us pray. Loving Father, you sent Jesus your only Son to die on the cross and to restore life through his Resurrection. Help us to see your love in his sacrifice. As we express our sorrow for sin, may we return to you in loving service. We ask this through your Son, who lives and loves with you and the Holy Spirit forever.

All: Amen

Leader: For the times we argue with one another,

Response: Lord have mercy.

Leader: For the times we fail to listen to one another,

Response: Lord have mercy.

Leader: For the times we take one another for granted,

Response: Lord have mercy.

Leader: For the times we put one another down,

Response: Lord have mercy.

Reader: Psalm 28:6-9

Leader: Let us pray. Merciful Lord, we thank you for the gift of your never-ending love. Through your sacrifice you have freed us from sin. Father, Son, and Holy Spirit, all glory and honor is yours today and forever.

All: Amen

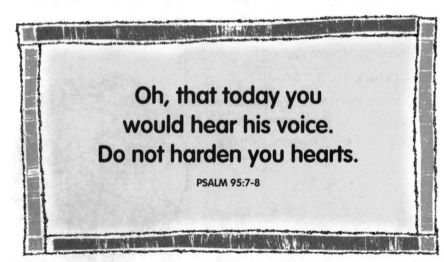

Oh, that today you would hear his voice. Do not harden you hearts.

PSALM 95:7-8

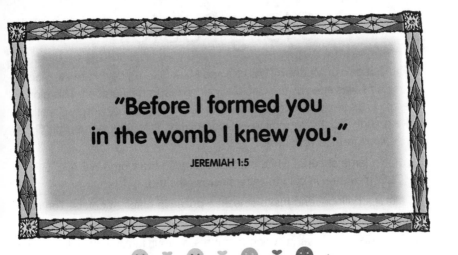

> # "Before I formed you in the womb I knew you."
>
> **JEREMIAH 1:5**

Personal Inventory

Talk about these questions together, one at a time. Give each person a chance to answer the questions. If others in the family see you differently than you see yourself, give them a chance to tell you why. Don't argue or be defensive about your traits. If any of them make you uncomfortable, silently pray for the grace to change, and thank God for the gift of insight into yourself and your family members.

1. When I'm coming home, am I eager to get there? Why? Why not?

2. How do I welcome family members when they come home? Would they know I'm glad to see them?

Gordon Willman

3. How do I feel when someone in my family sincerely compliments me? Do I make it a practice to compliment other members of my family?

4. When was the last time I hugged a family member for no particular reason except love?

Glory Poster

The Gospels of Matthew (17:1-10) and Mark (9:2-10) celebrate the glory of Jesus as he was seen by the disciples during his Transfiguration. This glory is reflected in the world around us, and in the faith and love of our fellow Christians. Make a Glory Poster to remind everyone who visits your home that God's glory shines forth in your lives.

1. Use a large sheet of white poster paper with the words WE ARE GOD'S GLORY written in colorful letters across the top.

2. Draw a balloon, and make at least a dozen in different colors. The more balloons you make, the more colorful your poster will be.

3. Now discuss ways in which members of your family can reflect God's glory, for example, love, helpfulness, charity, prayer, cheerfulness, and so forth.

4. Using magic markers or crayons, write these words on your balloons.

5. Select a spot for hanging your poster where visitors and family alike can be reminded of God's glory in your lives.

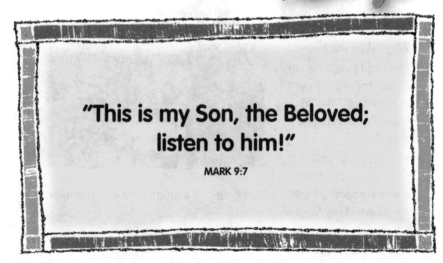

"This is my Son, the Beloved; listen to him!"

MARK 9:7

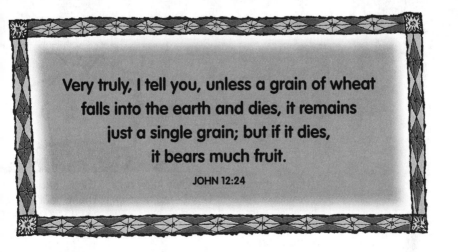

Very truly, I tell you, unless a grain of wheat falls into the earth and dies, it remains just a single grain; but if it dies, it bears much fruit.

JOHN 12:24

Tree of Life

Building a family tree is easy and can be very formal or very simple, large or small. You will need a large piece of paper or poster board, perhaps two feet by three feet or a similar size. You'll also need crayons or colored markers.

Draw the roots of the tree, and label them God the Creator, to remind your family that it is rooted in the Creator. Identify the trunk of the tree as Jesus; he is the anchor for the branches of the tree, the various members of the family. Draw branches for each member of the family. (If your family is small, you might include others: grandparents, uncles, aunts, close friends, neighbors.) Each member chooses a symbol to identify his or her branch. The symbol could relate to work outside the home, a hobby or interest, or something special for which the family member is known.

Under each branch, the other family members write a special quality or gift that person is to the family. Thus, if there are five members in your family, under each branch there would be four different statements. As Lent unfolds you might be able to list more qualities or gifts that emerge. Keep adding to the list.

When you pass by your Tree of Life, pause and reflect upon the gifts that each of your family members brings to the family. Near the end of Lent, see if you can identify gifts and qualities that your whole family shares.

FAMILY LENTEN CALENDAR

sunday	monday	tuesday
Jim Corbett		
Take time to compliment the homilist, cantor, lector, or greeter on how well they do their ministry.	Rejoice in being numbered among God's children.	Smile and say "Thank you!" to all the service people even if they aren't friendly.
Be extra helpful to one of your family members.	Forgive someone who hurt you.	Offer to help an older neighbor with a chore.
Write a letter or postcard to distant friends or family.	Pray for someone you know in your community who is in need of healing.	FAMILY DISCUSSION What is the special gift our family has?
Ask God's blessings for the person you like the least.	Pray for all the people in hospitals and nursing homes.	Smile at everyone you meet today.
Compliment every member of your family.	Give up something you want today for those who have less.	FAMILY DISCUSSION What does Lent mean to me?

wednesday	thursday	friday	saturday
ASH WEDNESDAY	FAMILY DISCUSSION Are we aware of the poor? What can we do to help the poor?	Think of a quality that you have that could be strengthened. Work on it during Lent.	Go without some snack or a soft drink today, and give the money saved to a charity.
Say "I'm sorry," to someone you've hurt.	Read together about a favorite saint, and something about them you would like to imitate.	Pray together Psalm 100.	Write a love note to your grandparents, aunt, uncle, or some older person.
Read together the readings for Sunday's liturgy.	Do something special for your family.	As a family, visit someone who has been shut in.	Take a walk together. Bring bags and pick up litter as you go.
Light a candle today, and pray that Christ, the light of the world, be with you.	FAMILY DISCUSSION Do you know someone who is really lonely? How can we help?	Make a list of all the blessings in your life. Show them at your family meal and give thanks.	Make your family meal a party today, celebrate your love for one another.
Pray for all the people who are tempted to give up.	FAMILY DISCUSSION What are some of the special gifts of family members?	As a family, visit someone who is sick.	Pray for all who are lonely.
Pray for all the people who are hungry today.	Parents: Hug your children. Children: Hug your parents.	FAMILY DISCUSSION Are we as a family taking care of God's creation? What more can we do?	

Jim Corbett

Easter Spice Ring

- 3 tablespoons shortening
- 1 cup sugar
- 1 teaspoon baking soda
- 1 can tomato soup
- 2 cups flour
- 1 teaspoon each of cinnamon, mace, nutmeg, and cloves
- 1 1/2 cups raisins or candied fruit peel

Cream shortening and sugar. Stir baking soda into soup. Sift flour and spices, and add to the mixture of creamed shortening and sugar. Stir well. Then add soup mixture and raisins. Mix well. Bake in a tube pan at 325 degrees for 35 minutes. Remove from pan and allow to cool.

Frost with the following:

4 tablespoons soft margarine or butter
1/4 teaspoon salt
1/2 pound confectioners' sugar
1/8 cup frozen orange juice concentrate, thawed

Cream margarine, add salt and a little of the sugar, and work together well. Add the rest of the sugar and the orange juice concentrate alternately, in small portions, mixing thoroughly until icing spreads easily.

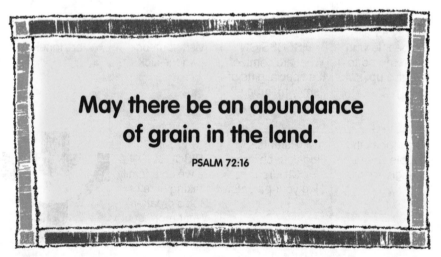

May there be an abundance of grain in the land.

PSALM 72:16

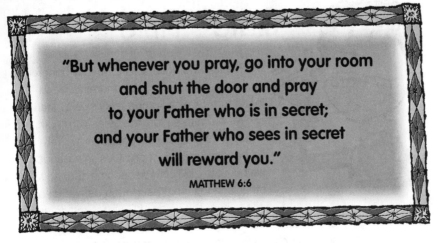

**"But whenever you pray, go into your room
and shut the door and pray
to your Father who is in secret;
and your Father who sees in secret
will reward you."**

MATTHEW 6:6

Lenten Prayer Partner

On Ash Wednesday, each family member should write his or her name on a piece of paper. Put the papers in a bowl, and have each person draw a name. This person becomes your Lenten Prayer Partner for the next six weeks. If you draw your own name, put it back and draw another. It is important that you keep the name of your secret friend a secret. Look for ways to give of yourself to your secret friend. Here are some suggestions.

- Offer to help with a job your Lenten Prayer Partner has to do.
- Write a note to your secret friend, telling him or her about the qualities or talents he or she has that you like. Don't sign the note.
- Compliment your Lenten Prayer Partner.
- Remember your Lenten Prayer Partner in your daily prayer, and pray for his or her intentions.
- Give your Lenten Prayer Partner a small gift.

During Holy Week, make a special Easter card for your Lenten Friend. You can make it out of construction paper and decorate it lavishly with signs of spring, the Resurrection, and new life. Include a loving message, and this time sign your name. On Easter morning, put your card at your secret friend's place. Finally, all will learn who has been their secret friend.

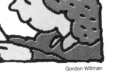

Gordon Willman

Quiet Time

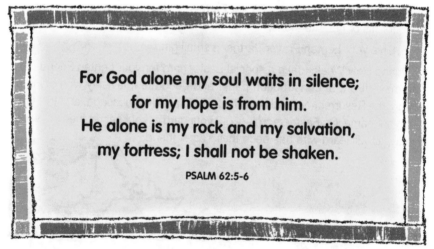

Silence and quiet are not readily honored in our Western culture. In the morning, how many of us turn on a radio or a television to start the day? We seem to equate the quiet with "nothing," or "absence" in a very negative way. Yet when we become quiet a marvelous thing happens: we begin to LISTEN! We become attuned to the other sounds which surround us; we also can listen within our hearts and spirits to hear the voice of God beckoning us and encouraging us, or perhaps challenging us.

As a family, see if you can set aside a short period of time each week in which you observe a period of quiet. No television, no radios or stereos, no computer games or web surfing, and no talking. It may be very hard to do this at first.

You may wish to create a simple family ritual, such as outlined below, to help formalize things.

1. Light a candle and gather in a circle or around the table.

2. Read a short passage from Scripture: 1 Kings 19:11-12; Psalm 62:1-2; Matthew 14:23.

3. Ask God to bless your time of quiet and silence. Thank God for the gift of Jesus and the gift of one another. Ask God's help in maintaining the quiet time.

4. Conclude by reciting the Lord's Prayer.

> **For God alone my soul waits in silence;**
> **for my hope is from him.**
> **He alone is my rock and my salvation,**
> **my fortress; I shall not be shaken.**
>
> **PSALM 62:5-6**

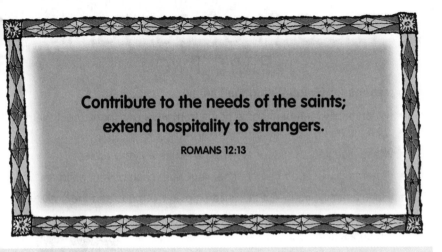

Contribute to the needs of the saints; extend hospitality to strangers.

ROMANS 12:13

The Gift of Our Family
PART ONE

Jesus has gifted us in these special ways to share his love with one another and with other people. When we share our gifts, we are sharing Jesus' love and his life. When we give the gift of ourselves, we are like Jesus because he gave himself to us. Like Jesus, when we give ourselves, the result is always new life for ourselves and for others.

What is the gift of your family? How can you best share that gift? Here are some suggestions:

Suggestions for Giving Outside of the Family

- Visit a member of your parish who is in a nursing home.
- Find out who needs a ride to Mass on Sundays, and offer them a ride.
- Who lives alone in your neighborhood? Pay him or her a visit or extend an invitation to dinner. (Don't be put off if they say "No," the first time. You may need to build up a relationship before he or she will feel comfortable coming over.)
- Offer to baby-sit for free for younger children in your neighborhood so their parents can have a night out.
- If someone in the neighborhood or parish is a caregiver for a loved one who has Alzheimer's disease or a chronic illness, offer to stay with that person so that the caregiver can have a day off.
- Spend a day building people up. Make a point to affirm people and thank them.

The Gift of Our Family
PART TWO

Suggestions for Giving Within the Family

- When family members come home from work or school, greet them with a big hug.
- Make cleaning a room or area of the house a family project.
- Parents, try to spend some time alone with each of your children.
- Have a family night—let the children plan the menu and the activity.
- Offer to help with the laundry or putting the groceries away.
- Smile at other family members.
- Play a game with a younger sister or brother.
- Clean your room before you are reminded to do so.
- Go to bed without a fuss or delay.
- Write a letter or send an e-mail to a friend who has been waiting to hear from you.
- Compliment your dad, mom, sister, brother on their special qualities.
- Remember the magic words: please, thank-you, you're welcome, and I'm sorry.

And whatever you do, in word or deed, do everything in the name of the Lord Jesus, giving thanks to God the Father through him.

COLOSSIANS 3:17

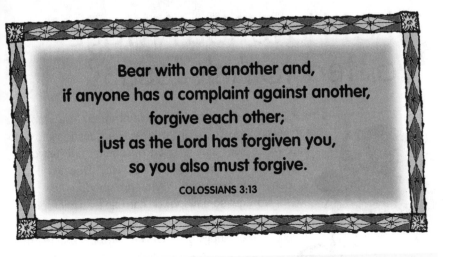

Bear with one another and,
if anyone has a complaint against another,
forgive each other;
just as the Lord has forgiven you,
so you also must forgive.

COLOSSIANS 3:13

A Family Celebration of Reconciliation
Two

1. Have each family member read a portion of a Bible passage on reconciliation, perhaps the parable of the prodigal son (Luke 15:11-32). If the children are able and time permits, a short discussion may be helpful.

2. Invite each family member to write on a card or paper one behavior for which they are sorry. Include a line stating what you plan to do to change this behavior. Using either a fireplace, or a candle and an aluminum pie plate, burn each paper as a sign of letting go of that behavior and /or the guilt attached to it.

3. After burning the papers, someone start an act of contrition with each family member adding a line or two to the prayer. If your family is not comfortable with this, say a traditional act of contrition together.

4. On the positive side, the family can decide on one step they could take to make more peace in the home, and one thing they could do together for reconciliation in the wider community.

5. A big family hug is a wonderful, tangible expression of reconciliation. The whole service can be concluded with a special family dinner or treat (at home or out).

What Have You Always Wanted to Ask Jesus?

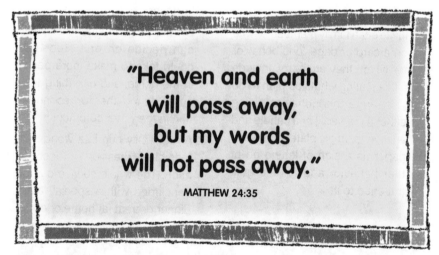

Pretend you're an important news reporter. You want to interview Jesus. Think up at least five questions to ask him. Make sure they're good questions, not just ones that can be answered "Yes" or "No." Questions that begin with "How" and "Why" are good.

Now get something you can use for a microphone (a spoon is good). Then, get your mom, dad, or some other adult to pretend they're Jesus. Tell this person you're a reporter for GNN (The Good News Network). Ask this person if he or she would answer your questions the way Jesus might answer.

When you've finished, switch places and let the grownups ask you five questions they've always wanted to ask Jesus. Then *you* answer the way you think that Jesus might respond.

Jim Corbett

"Heaven and earth
will pass away,
but my words
will not pass away."

MATTHEW 24:35

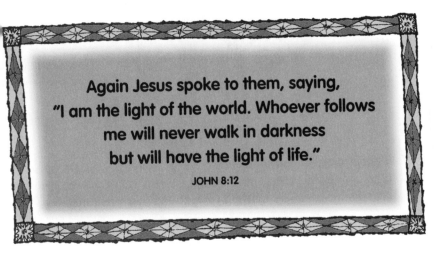

Again Jesus spoke to them, saying,
"I am the light of the world. Whoever follows
me will never walk in darkness
but will have the light of life."

JOHN 8:12

Easter Candle

At the beginning of Lent you may have devoted some family time to making candles. Use one of them, or make a new one. (If you did not do this activity or prefer not to do it, then purchase a large pillar candle or see if you have one on hand.) Decorate your candle with a cross.

On Holy Saturday, during your family prayer time, stick five whole cloves into your candle in the form of a cross. (You will have to first use a pin to carefully make five holes so that it will be easier to insert the cloves.) The cloves represent the five wounds of Christ. Say this prayer while putting the cloves into the candle: ***By his wounds, holy and glorious, may he who is Christ the Lord protect and preserve us.*** Light the candle, and have each member of the family offer a short prayer of praise or thanksgiving.

Light your Easter Candle on Easter morning. Keep it on your dining room table during the season of Easter, and light it whenever the family gathers for food and prayer. May it continue to remind you that Christ, the Light of the world, has risen.

Chris Sharp

Roots

Talk about these questions together, one at a time. Give each person a chance to answer the questions. Respect the feelings of one another, and thank God for the gifts of insight into yourself and your family members.

1. How do I feel about our family praying together?

2. If Jesus was a guest in our home for dinner, would I act differently?

3. Christ is present in all the members of my family. How does that make me feel? How does each family member remind me of Christ?

4. What do I like best about being a member of this family?

Chris Sharp

Let your speech always be gracious, seasoned with salt, so that you may know how you ought to answer everyone.

COLOSSIANS 4:6

34

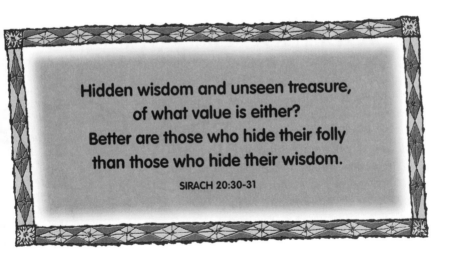

Hidden wisdom and unseen treasure,
of what value is either?
Better are those who hide their folly
than those who hide their wisdom.

SIRACH 20:30-31

Things Bag

1. Place a number of objects in a pillowcase, and hang it so that it's within reach of everyone. (All get to contribute a few items to the pillowcase; don't let the others see what you are putting inside!) Gather ordinary household items, like a toothbrush, a comb, a pencil. (Don't put any fragile items in the bag.) Don't fill it too full. Make a list of what you put in the bag, fold it, and put it in a small container.

2. Take turns feeling the free-hanging pillowcase for a few minutes. (Depending upon the range of ages, you may want to set an arbitrary amount of time for this.) After your turn at the pillowcase, write down all the things you think are inside.

3. When everyone is finished, compare lists with the combined list of items in the bag. The person who guesses correctly the most items wins a small prize or is excused from doing his or her household chores for that week.

Sacrifice and Sharing

As a family, discuss and decide different ways members could make sacrifices during Lent that would save money. Some examples are skipping or reducing snacks, soda, and liquor; simpler meals or occasional "poverty meals"; less frequent and less expensive entertainment; reduced energy consumption at home and while driving.

Gordon Willman

Each week, as you meet together to acknowledge the sacrifices and pool the money each member has saved, place the money in a special container.

Decide together on some recipients of your sacrificial savings. Earmark some of the money for a world-wide provider like Catholic Relief Services, Operation Rice Bowl, or Holy Childhood's World Bank, that suggests our connectedness to our brothers and sisters all over the world.

You may prefer to give to a local organization that assists the needy. Perhaps you may wish to choose two groups, one international and one local, and alternate weeks or simply split the combined savings at the end of Lent. You may also wish to consider groups like Bread for the World or Pax Christi.

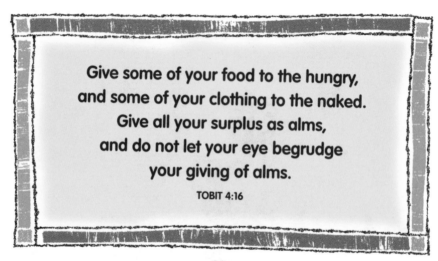

Give some of your food to the hungry,
and some of your clothing to the naked.
Give all your surplus as alms,
and do not let your eye begrudge
your giving of alms.

TOBIT 4:16

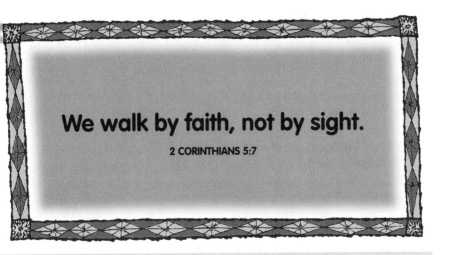

We walk by faith, not by sight.

2 CORINTHIANS 5:7

We Remember

As Christians, we believe that, like Jesus, we will go through the paschal mystery many times in our own lives and one final time at the moment of our death.

- Spend some time reflecting on those who have been close to you that have died and are now with the Lord.

- Slowly read this Scripture passage:
  But the souls of the righteous are in the hand of God, and no torment will ever touch them. In the eyes of the foolish they seemed to have died, and their departure was thought to be a disaster, and their going from us to be their destruction; but they are at peace. Wisdom 3:1-3

- Remember someone close to you who has died. Bring this person's image into your mind's eye. As you remember this life, imagine the Lord Jesus escorting him or her into heaven at the time of death. Finally, imagine this loved one waiting for you. Know that when your time of passing comes, the Lord and your loved ones who have gone before you will escort you into the kingdom of heaven.

- Finish your short remembering with this prayer:
  Lord, you are the resurrection and the life.
  If anyone believes in you,
  even though they die they will live.
  Whoever believes in you will never die.
  Lord, through the power of your rising,
  help me believe in my own resurrection.
  Amen

"Seeing" the Body of Christ

Roger von Oech, in his book, *A Kick in the Seat of the Pants*, suggests, "Take a look around where you're sitting and find five things that have blue in them." (Go ahead and do it.)

With a "blue" mind-set, you'll find that blue jumps out at you; a blue book on the table, a blue cushion on the couch, blue in the painting on the wall, and so on. In like fashion, you've probably noticed that after you buy a new car you see that make of car everywhere. That's because people find what they are looking for.

We may think it ludicrous to expect to "see" God. Yet we simply lack a "God" mind-set. When we develop our sensitivity, we soon begin to see God everywhere, in all things, and most important, in every person. In this way, then, we "see" the body of Christ and become not only responsible TO it, but responsible FOR it.

Try for at least one day to see each person you meet as the body of Christ, even those people who are difficult or challenging to deal with. Remind yourself that sometimes the body of Christ is wounded and broken; see where you can be an instrument of healing.

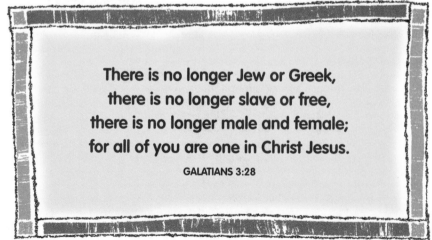

There is no longer Jew or Greek,
there is no longer slave or free,
there is no longer male and female;
for all of you are one in Christ Jesus.

GALATIANS 3:28

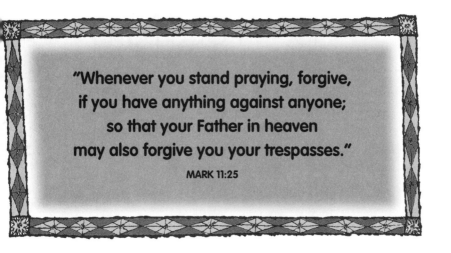

"Whenever you stand praying, forgive,
if you have anything against anyone;
so that your Father in heaven
may also forgive you your trespasses."

MARK 11:25

Reconciliation and Repentance

Have each family member read a portion of a Bible passage on reconciliation such as:

Matthew 5:23-24
(Be reconciled before offering your gift at the altar)

Luke 15:11-32
(Prodigal Son)

Matthew 18:21-25
(How many times must I forgive?)

Then discuss these questions:

1. Do I make an effort to see the members of my family as good?

2. Do I speak kindly yet openly about what I think and feel?

3. Do I tell individual members what I like about them?

4. Do I try to resolve conflicts or do I rush to make judgement?

5. Am I careful about the use of other's property?

6. Am I open to sharing prayer as a family?

Decide on one step that you could take to make more peace in your own home, and one thing the family could do together for reconciliation in the wider community.

Hot Cross Buns

Ingredients:

1 package yeast	1/4 cup butter or margarine
1/4 cup warm water	3 3/4 cups flour
1 cup milk	1 egg
1 teaspoon salt	1/2 teaspoon cinnamon
1/4 cup sugar	1/2 cup raisins

Dissolve the yeast in warm water.

Scald the milk. Remove from heat, and add salt, sugar, and butter. Cool. Stir in 1 cup of flour, beating until smooth. Add the dissolved yeast. Stir in egg, cinnamon, and raisins. Mix well.

Stir in remaining flour, making a soft dough. Turn out onto a floured surface, and knead for about five minutes. Grease the inside of a large bowl with shortening. Place the kneaded dough in it, and turn the dough until it is completely coated with shortening. Cover with a towel, and place in a warm spot until doubled in size (about 90 minutes). Punch down. Turn out onto a floured surface, and let it rest for ten minutes. Shape into buns, and place on a greased baking sheet, one inch apart. Cover and place in a warm spot till they double (about 30 minutes). Bake in an oven preheated to 375 degrees until golden brown (about 15-20 minutes). Cool on racks.

Frosting ingredients

1 cup confectioners sugar

Enough milk to make a semi-thick frosting

Frost your cooled buns with crosses. Enjoy them on Easter morning, as you celebrate the gift of new life in the Resurrection of the Lord.

> **When the sabbath was over, Mary Magdalene, and Mary the mother of James, and Salome bought spices, so that they might go and anoint him.**
>
> **MARK 16:1**

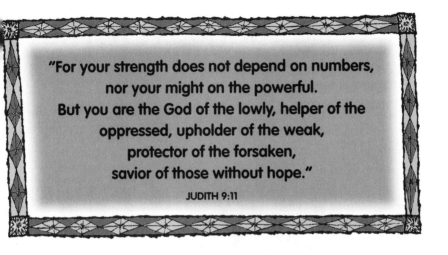

"For your strength does not depend on numbers,
nor your might on the powerful.
But you are the God of the lowly, helper of the
oppressed, upholder of the weak,
protector of the forsaken,
savior of those without hope."

JUDITH 9:11

People of Conviction

As individuals and as a family we are called to act with conviction. A good family lenten practice is to gather your family together once a week, go through the daily newspaper, and identify people of conviction.

1. Cut out articles that show people acting with conviction.

2. Glue these articles on a piece of poster board. OR, if you have a computer and scanner, scan them, and create a collage on the computer. If you have Internet access, you can pull stories directly off the Web about people who act with conviction.

3. After you glue each article on the board, have each person in the family write around the border of the article how he or she would act in this situation. If you used a computer to generate your collage, print the collage, and then have family members write their responses down. At a family meal, discuss your responses.

4. Post your collage on a bulletin board or refrigerator, to provide family members' inspiration.

Family Service Activity

1. Dye Easter eggs to take to a shelter for women and children so they can have an Easter egg hunt together.

2. Write a family letter to government leaders on behalf of the hungry.

3. Make Easter cards/greetings for a relative, friend, prisoner, or others needing encouragement.

4. Gather toys, food, clothes, or personal care items for the poor.

5. Assist a single mother or an elderly person with spring housecleaning.

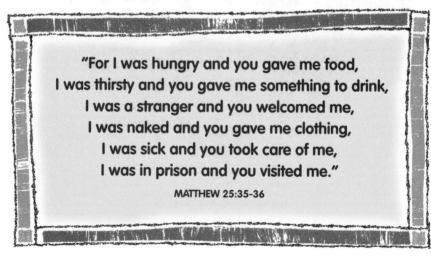

"For I was hungry and you gave me food,
I was thirsty and you gave me something to drink,
I was a stranger and you welcomed me,
I was naked and you gave me clothing,
I was sick and you took care of me,
I was in prison and you visited me."

MATTHEW 25:35-36

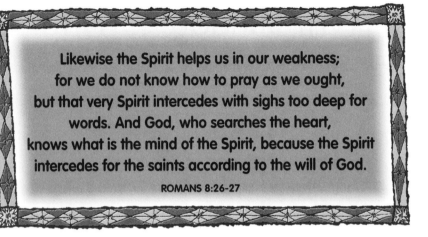

> Likewise the Spirit helps us in our weakness;
> for we do not know how to pray as we ought,
> but that very Spirit intercedes with sighs too deep for
> words. And God, who searches the heart,
> knows what is the mind of the Spirit, because the Spirit
> intercedes for the saints according to the will of God.
>
> **ROMANS 8:26-27**

Six Family Prayer Ideas

1. Make bedtime forgiveness time. That's the time to forgive or say, "I'm sorry," for bad things that have happened during the day. End with a touch, a hug, or a kiss.

2. Tell the story of a patron saint of different family members.

3. Sprinkle holy water at bedtime before saying "good-night."

4. At bedtime, light a special candle, and gather the family on or around your child's bed. (If you have more than one child, rotate the location.) Each person say a prayer or blessing for the family.

Bill Wittman

5. Bedtime is a good time for the wonderful story of "how you were born," "how we met and fell in love," "good people we know," and so forth.

6. Try a special family meal at the end of each week. Make it a celebration each time by taking turns recalling one good thing that happened since the last meal.

Palm Sunday Activity

Make sure that each family member receives a palm. When you arrive at home, everyone should place the palm somewhere special in his or her room. You could use this prayer as you put the palm in its special place:

Lord, today we begin the
most sacred week of the church year.
May this palm remind us of your victory over sin
and death. Help us to see your face
in the suffering of others and allow us
to walk with them. Amen

Then those who went ahead and those
who followed were shouting,
"Hosanna! Blessed is the one who
comes in the name of the Lord!
Blessed is the coming kingdom of our ancestor David!
Hosanna in the highest heaven!"

MARK 11:9-10

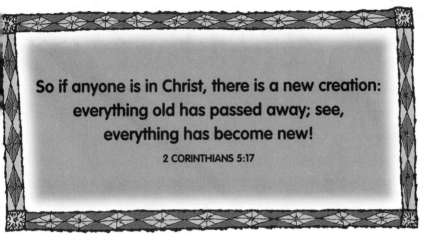

> So if anyone is in Christ, there is a new creation:
> everything old has passed away; see,
> everything has become new!
>
> **2 CORINTHIANS 5:17**

Dyeing Easter Eggs with Natural Dyes

You will need the following:

- Eggs
- Vinegar
- Water

For the natural colors you will need:

- orange peels = light yellow
- pear peelings = chartreuse
- onion skins = orange
- coffee = brown
- cabbage = blue-red
- cranberries = purple

1. Add each ingredient to its own pot of water, and bring each mixture to a hardy boil.
2. Add the eggs and a teaspoon of vinegar. Be sure that there is enough water in the pot to cover the eggs.
3. Reduce the heat so they will bubble very slowly. Cook approximately 20 minutes.
4. Remove the eggs from the water with a spoon, and place them on a towel or rack so that they can safely cool.

Family Station:

A traditional Catholic devotion, the Stations of the Cross are often pra
privately by individuals, and during Lent they are often prayed as a group.
often see the fourteen or fifteen stations on the walls of our parish churc
but we tend to view them more as works of art than as a formal prayer.

One way to make the Stations of the Cross come alive for your family i
think about them in terms of the world in which we live today. Who are
ones who are condemned in today's world? Where have we seen the fa
Jesus in today's world?

Write out the Stations of the Cross on slips of paper, and put them in a

1. Jesus is condemned to death
2. Jesus takes up his cross
3. Jesus falls for the first time
4. Jesus meets his mother
5. Simon helps Jesus

6. Veronica wipes the face of Jesus
7. Jesus falls for the second time
8. Jesus meets the crying women
9. Jesus falls for the third time
10. Jesus is stripped of his clothing

f the Cross

ntainer. Have each member of the family draw one (or more) of the Stations.
member of the family is to find a situation in our contemporary world that
cts their Station. Then conclude with a prayer for those people who make
ur "station."

r example: The First Station: Jesus is Condemned to Death. Like Jesus,
are many men and women who are unjustly condemned throughout the
d. They wait out their sentences sometimes in fear of their lives, sometimes
a grim resignation that they may never leave their cells. Oh God, we pray
l prisoners, for their families and for their loved ones. Help us to remember
they are your children too.

11. Jesus is nailed to the cross
12. Jesus dies on the cross
13. Jesus is taken down from the cross
14. Jesus is buried on the cross
15. The Resurrection

**But we proclaim Christ crucified,
a stumbling block to Jews and
foolishness to Gentiles.**

1 CORINTHIANS 1:23

When it was the
evening on that day,
the first day of the week,
and the doors of the
house where the
disciples had met

were locked for fear
of the Jews,
Jesus came and stoo⌐
among them and sai⌐
"Peace be with you."
John 20

Liguori
One Liguori Drive
Liguori MO 63057-9999
$1.95

Jim Corbett

ISBN 0-7648-0704-8

50195>

9 780764 807046   37135